INNER PEACE

INNER PEACE

A GUIDED
MEDITATION JOURNAL
for beginners

JORDANA REIM

ROCKRIDGE
PRESS

For general information on our other products and services or to obtain technical support, please contact our Customer Care Department within the United States at (866) 744-2665, or outside the United States at (510) 253-0500.

Rockridge Press publishes its books in a variety of electronic and print formats. Some content that appears in print may not be available in electronic books, and vice versa.

TRADEMARKS: Rockridge Press and the Rockridge Press logo are trademarks or registered trade-marks of Callisto Media Inc. and/or its affiliates, in the United States and other countries, and may not be used without written permission. All other trademarks are the property of their respective owners. Rockridge Press is not associated with any product or vendor mentioned in this book.

Art Director: Jennifer Hsu

Art Producer: Hannah Dickerson

Editors: Emily Angell and Claire Yee

Production Manager: Riley Hoffman

Production Editor: Ruth Sakata Corley

Cover and interior art, Creative Market

Author photo courtesy of Michi Carlessi

ISBN: Print 978-1-64611-926-4

R0

FOR MOM, DAD, AND AVIVA.
FOR UNDERSTANDING
MY UNORTHODOX PATH,
CHEERING ME ON, AND
CELEBRATING EVERY TIME
I COME BACK TO THE USA.
I LOVE YOU.

FOR PAULINE.

THIS JOURNAL BELONGS TO:

WHEN I LET GO OF
WHAT I AM, I BECOME
WHAT I MIGHT BE.

Lao Tzu

CONTENTS

INTRODUCTION

Committing yourself to meditation and journaling is a big step toward self-exploration, reflection, and growth. Some people go months, years, or an entire lifetime without taking a deeper look at themselves.

It can be demoralizing to strive for peace and realize you aren't where you want to be. I've been there, and I've come to terms with the idea that I'll always be a work in progress. It's important to remember that growth doesn't happen overnight—self-exploration is a never-ending exercise! I've learned that when you find peace in the process, you find progress in unexpected ways, sometimes even faster than you think possible.

Four years ago, I wasn't teaching meditation. I was an executive producer in Los Angeles. I'd spent over ten years in the industry and my career was at a high, but I felt conflicted—for years my heart and my work weren't in alignment. I knew there was something else for me, but I was scared to leave my financially secure and familiar grounds.

The greatest peace I found was in my morning meditations. Every day before heading to work, I'd wake up early to meditate, practice gratitude, and journal. Through these practices, I came to a place of inner security and peace that led me to leave my job and practice meditation full time. Over the next few years, I traveled to India, Thailand, Nepal, Cambodia, and Bali, studying meditation, yoga, and thought transformation with great teachers while also studying myself in meditation, inquiry, and writing.

I lived in monasteries and ashrams and sought opportunities to teach as I learned, which I found deepened my own practice. I was profoundly changed and inspired through a role I had teaching meditation and yoga to students with critical illnesses and cancer. While helping these students navigate the uncertainty of sickness and death, I realized the importance of meeting any circumstance with loving acceptance, peace, and equanimity.

These days, I guide group and private meditation sessions primarily in my home city of Santa Monica, though as I write this I'm in Nepal on the heels of guiding a ten-day spiritual retreat in the Himalayas. Reflection and meditation have taken me to new heights in four years, but it still takes writing it down for me to realize my own personal and professional growth.

This book is a product of that learning. I have seen that even short practices of meditation, journaling, and reflection can be life changing, whether your life takes a 180-degree turn as mine did or you're simply able to find more space between troubling interactions and your reactions. I have found with my students that even after a few sessions of meditation and reflection, they experience transformations in how they think and act in their lives.

A student of mine, Rick, travels often to visit building projects and look at prospective investments. He wanted to work through the anxiety he experienced while traveling. A few weeks into our meditation sessions, Rick had a layover in Hong Kong that turned into a twenty-four-hour delay. Normally, Rick would have thrown money at the problem, arranged another flight to his destination, and festered in anger for a week. However, in this instance, Rick decided to let the situation be and chose to explore Hong Kong with a sense of curiosity and playfulness. Since he chose to find peace with the situation rather than force an outcome, Rick remained collected throughout the flight delay, and he reaped the benefits of that calm mind-set with an influx of productivity.

I want to help you find your breakthrough! This book includes a variety of meditations, affirmations, mantras, inspiring quotes, intentions, and powerful prompts to help you start and reflect on your own practice. The quotes and prompts will inspire you to keep going when the practice gets difficult and progress seems slow.

While meditation and journaling are great ways to get inspired, relieve stress, and manage anxiety, this book is not a replacement for a therapist, medication, or medical treatment. If you have ongoing or debilitating issues, don't hesitate to see a medical professional. There is no shame in seeking this help, and it pairs well with the reflection practices that support your overall well-being.

As you progress through this journal, you'll record the insights you have during the meditations in the blank writing spaces provided. Even simple practices can spark something spectacular within you. You'll discover new things about yourself and find that peace will meet you wherever you are.

It's great to be on this journey with you!

With gratitude for you,

Jordana

Meditation for Beginners

There's a lot of doing that happens in not-doing. As you begin your journey with meditation, you'll find a balance between not-doing and doing. Through this, you will deepen your experience of self-knowledge, gleaning personal growth and insights. You'll learn many ways to find a meditative, peaceful state in which reflections come more naturally. Some practices in this book will feel better than others. Explore why that is by doing each meditation at least three times. This book is a progression, but also an exploration: What helps you learn more about yourself? What guides you to peace and what challenges you the most?

Why You Should Meditate

It's no wonder why the words *meditation* and *medicine* share the same root. The benefits of meditation are vast and can feel like medicine for your soul. Here are just a few reasons to include meditation in your regular routine:

It helps relieve stress. Meditation is an opportunity to interrupt what's stressing you out and reset your nervous system. It's like hitting pause on tension and hitting play on peace.

It clears your mind. Ever feel like the same (mostly negative) thoughts keep swirling through your head? Meditation sweeps away mind clutter and creates space for clarity and deep thoughts.

It forces you to be in the moment. Meditation is a practice in presence. It's likely that your daily thoughts are focused on the past or the future. In time, you will increase your ability to live in and savor the present moment.

It fosters forgiveness and letting go. We often hold on to anger or resentment and then, over time, forget that they are buried under layers of other thoughts and memories in our minds. Meditation helps you let go of resentments, anger, and other feelings that do not serve you, so you can experience each day with a more peaceful mind.

It improves cognitive function. Meditation helps you focus and supports your ability to see the bigger picture of any experience without reacting in haste. Once you incorporate this practice into your daily routine, you'll find that it sharpens your perception, increases your calm, and gives you a heightened ability to make smart choices and react with rational responses.

It results in a better night's sleep. When you meditate, you quiet the thoughts that previously occupied the rooms of your mind. With decreased levels of stress and a heart filled with forgiveness and peace, you will enjoy more restorative and rejuvenating sleep at night.

How to Meditate

Getting started with anything new has its challenges. Meditation seems simple, so it can be frustrating if you feel like you don't "get it" right away. Here are a few tips to make things easier as you begin your practice.

Find a quiet place. Make sure you meditate in a place where you feel comfortable and won't be interrupted. You'll want to have a timer and something on which to sit or lie down. It may be helpful in the beginning to use an app such as Insight Timer, Simple Habit, or Unplug Meditation, which allow you to stream several guided meditations for free.

Get comfortable. Find a pose that's most comfortable for you. Unless you have a medical condition that prevents you from doing so, it's best to do meditations sitting up with a straight spine so you remain awake and alert. You can sit cross-legged on a cushion on the floor, or in a chair with your feet planted firmly on the ground.

Keep your hands still. While there are many mudras (hand positions) in meditation, it's best to keep it simple in the beginning. Place the back of your left hand inside the palm of your right hand in your lap, or rest your hands on your thighs, palms facing up or down.

Stay focused. It's common for beginners to fall asleep during their practice. If you're feeling sleepy, move around before beginning your meditation. Shake your body or do some exercise. When you meditate, instead of lying down, practice sitting up and lengthening your spine, allowing energy to move easily from your root to your crown. It's best to practice on an empty stomach or, at the very least, not after a big meal.

Why You Should Keep a Meditation Journal

Keeping a meditation journal is like having a good friend who moves you toward accelerated insight and growth. If you hold yourself accountable for your journey and your journaling, you can experience profound transformation. Here are a few reasons why you should keep a meditation journal.

Keep track of your progress. When you see your reflections in this journal's pages, you'll have a visual gauge of how much you've completed. Read your past entries, try meditations again, and see how your practice has shifted or what more you can uncover.

Record your experience. An experience is a sliver of life. By recording how you felt during a meditation, you can enhance your life, deepening your awareness of the experience and reflecting on it or savoring what you find.

Write down your challenges, successes, and everything in between. Inner peace blooms when you meet yourself wherever you are on any given day in any given moment. Some days feel effortless; others feel challenging. Some practices will resonate with you; others will be harder for you to grasp. By acknowledging and recording your challenges and successes, you can understand the multidimensional nature of you and begin to find peace with the ups, downs, and inevitable changes from moment to moment and practice to practice.

Take note of your insights, reflections, and breakthroughs. Meditation is a powerful practice that can dredge up buried thoughts, memories, and insights. Giving your mind the opportunity to be still creates a new pathway for deeper thoughts to surface. By journaling as part of your practice, you can be sure to remember these insights and breakthroughs, giving yourself the opportunity to reflect and pivot from where you've been to where you want to go, personally, professionally, and in your relationships with others.

How to Use This Journal

This journal is a guide to help support you as you deepen your practice of personal reflection. It's meant to be insightful and enjoyable. Once you begin your meditation journey, you'll need to play a role in deciding what works best for you. It's important that you find a personal rhythm that keeps you motivated and excited, so meditation never feels like a chore.

Start by choosing and completing one of the meditations in this book. (Although this journal is organized in a progressive way, you don't have to start at the beginning if you don't want to.) Then, read the associated writing prompts and decide whether you want to write answers to every prompt all in one sitting or if it feels better to focus on one prompt at a time. It's best if you stick with a meditation for a minimum of three days before moving into a new practice, so, if you like, you can answer a new prompt each time you complete the meditation. If you really enjoy a particular meditation, feel free to repeat it more than three days in a row, increasing the time you spend with it each day. The writing prompts included with each meditation will help you reflect on how the practice felt for you and how you can use the technique to feel more centered and at peace. Through these written reflections, you will address universal and personal issues pertaining to four major themes: inner peace (part 1), mental focus (part 2), reacting to and overcoming obstacles (part 3), and gratitude and forgiveness (part 4). Along the way, you'll find intentions, affirmations, and quotes in each section of the book that will inspire you to take action and carry what you have learned through meditation into your daily life.

Take a moment to cleanse yourself of previous assumptions and look at yourself and your life with a renewed state of wonder. If you ever get frustrated with your progress with meditation, try to meet yourself with kindness—it's not easy, but I assure you, you're always making progress when you practice. Set yourself up for success by practicing regularly—schedule a time or times of day that work best for you to meditate.

Ready, set, let's sit! Your journey in begins now.

DO NOT WAIT UNTIL
THE CONDITIONS ARE
PERFECT TO BEGIN.
BEGINNING MAKES THE
CONDITIONS PERFECT.

Alan Cohen

Part One

FIND INNER PEACE

It's easy to lose your center of peace in the busyness of routines, obligations, and to-dos. This is further exacerbated by your ever-changing interpersonal relationships, emotions, body, and mind. The good news is that peace is within you and always available. With practice—even in the midst of chaos— you can access your inner peace when you need it most.

Contrary to popular belief, you won't find inner peace by turning a blind eye to triggers or bothersome emotions like sadness or resentment, nor by searching for happiness. Peace is a balanced state in which you allow all that you notice in the present moment to be as it is. Peace doesn't require you to change an emotion you're feeling. Peace asks for presence and withholding judgment, good and bad.

Each of the following meditations will help you find peace as you embrace all aspects of who you are. Acceptance of yourself and your experience in the present moment is the key to your sanctuary of ever-blooming inner peace.

IF WE ARE PEACEFUL,

IF WE ARE HAPPY, WE CAN

SMILE, AND EVERYONE IN

OUR FAMILY, OUR ENTIRE

SOCIETY, WILL BENEFIT

FROM OUR PEACE.

Thich Nhat Hanh

Find Your Center

Meditation

1. Find a comfortable way to sit. Let your palms face upward with the backs of your hands resting on your thighs.

2. Relax your body and face. Loosen your jaw. Gently close your eyes.

3. Take three deep breaths, feeling your belly fill up on your inhale and slowly deflate on your exhale. Let your breathing settle into its natural rhythm.

4. Think about the center of calm in your body. Where does your intuition tell you this place is? Bring your awareness to this place and observe as your breath goes there. Imagine your breath flowing in and out of your center.

5. As you breathe into your center, imagine you are breathing in the energy of peace. As you breathe out, imagine that this peace is beaming out from your center.

Writing Prompts

Where in your body did you locate your center? Did this surprise you? Why?

_____

_____

_____

_____

_____

_____

Describe how it felt when you breathed in the energy of peace. Can you imagine your peace beaming out into your life? Is there an area of your life or a relationship where you want to send this peace?

_____

_____

_____

_____

_____

_____

_____

Reflect on a recent or prominent memory in which you lost your center.

_____

_____

_____

_____

_____

_____

Is there a person in your life who triggers you? How might centering your peace change how you approach this person the next time you see them? Describe how you'd like the next encounter to be rooted in peace.

_____

_____

_____

_____

_____

_____

_____

Are there certain times or situations in which you think centering your peace would be most beneficial for you? At your job? When you interact with certain people who trigger you? List these times, situations, or people and explain why you need to approach each one with peace.

Set an Intention

Repeat these words in your mind: "I am breathing
peace in. I am breathing peace out."

Become aware if you feel off-center during
the day. Take a moment to close your eyes and
breathe peace into your center.

PEACE COMES

FROM WITHIN.

DO NOT SEEK IT

WITHOUT.

Buddha

Space for Peace

Meditation

1. Before you start a new task or difficult conversation, take a moment to pause.

2. Sit taller, let your spine be long, and relax your shoulders. Softly close your eyes.

3. In your mind, recall silently something that you have completed: "I just finished an e-mail." Then tell yourself, "I am making space for peace."

4. Enjoy three deep breaths. Hold each inhale at the top for a count of four. Exhale and sigh the breath out of your mouth. Let your jaw be loose here. On your third breath, bring the corners of your lips toward your ears for a smile.

5. Keep your smile and, as you're ready, open your eyes, bringing the peace from your pause into your next activity.

Writing Prompts

How did this exercise of pausing in between tasks feel for you? Did you feel more present? Alert? Peaceful? Easeful?

Do you remember a time when you felt a sense of palpable peace while doing an everyday task? When was it? What were you doing?

Is there something that you find yourself routinely doing in an unconscious way? For example, do you unconsciously consume entire bags of chips or watch Netflix when you need to be sleeping? Are you present when you greet people you see regularly, or do you have an unconscious way of saying hello and moving past them?

How could pausing to make space for peace in between tasks support breaking an unconscious habit?

Reflect on how your day might go if you brought the space for peace into what you have ahead of you.

Set an Intention

Read this simple affirmation out loud three times:

"Today I will make space for peace through simple pauses. I will interrupt unconscious patterns with peace."

EVERY TIME YOU ARE

TEMPTED TO REACT IN THE

SAME OLD WAY, ASK IF YOU

WANT TO BE A PRISONER OF

THE PAST OR A PIONEER OF

THE FUTURE.

Deepak Chopra

Peace in Nature

Meditation

1. Spend a minimum of three to five minutes walking outside in nature. If you're in a big city, find a park to walk through.

2. Walk more slowly and quietly than you normally do. Savor the environment and notice what part of nature stands out for you (let it be something in the natural environment: a leaf, a flower, a tree, a rock, etc.).

3. Take a moment to sit or stand comfortably with the piece of nature that captures you. For thirty seconds or up to one minute, fix your attention on this object. Explore its color, textures, shape, scent, and how it feels when you touch it.

4. Allow your breath to be long and deep. Imagine you could be rooted like a tree here—stable and grounded—with what you've discovered.

5. Take a deep breath and exhale with a sigh. Smile. Repeat the process with another part of nature that captures you.

Writing Prompts

What attracted you to the object(s) of nature that stood out to you?

_____

_____

_____

_____

_____

_____

What do you notice about your piece(s) of nature? Did anything surprise you about what you noticed?

_____

_____

_____

_____

_____

_____

_____

How did it feel to pause and be rooted with your object(s) in nature? Can you recall a time when you felt connected to nature as a child? Relax into the memory. Write about what you remember.

What is your favorite way to enjoy nature? Reflect on the last time you did this.

_____

_____

_____

_____

_____

_____

Is there a place in nature you want to visit? It could be a place you've been before or one you dream of visiting on a day trip or destination vacation. What inspires you the most about visiting this place?

_____

_____

_____

_____

_____

_____

Set an Intention

Pay attention when you see pieces of nature outside their natural environments, and take a moment to appreciate them. Some examples of this are cut flowers, crystals in a home, seashells, or potted plants in an office. Recognize that this piece of nature has been relocated for your enjoyment. Let it remind you of your favorite pastimes in nature.

IF WE COULD SEE

THE MIRACLE OF A

SINGLE FLOWER CLEARLY,

OUR WHOLE LIFE

WOULD CHANGE.

Buddha

Soft Gaze of Peace

Meditation

1. Find a place to sit where you can remain mostly undisturbed, and sit upright in a comfortable position. Rest your hands gently in your lap and take a few full, grounding breaths.

2. Set a timer for three to five minutes.

3. Look straight ahead. Your eyes should feel both relaxed and aware as you fix your gaze on a single unmoving point ahead. Your eyelids should be half closed.

4. Without moving your head or eyes, notice your peripheral vision. Let that help you soften your eyes as you look ahead. Keep breathing as you normally would. If anything moves in your field of vision, resist the urge to follow it with your eyes. If you waiver, gently bring your gaze back and relax into your soft gaze of peace again.

5. When the timer goes off, close your eyes and enjoy the steadiness you've achieved. Bring your hands into the namaste position, your palms together and your thumbs at your heart. Take a moment to recognize the peace you've created.

Writing Prompts

Describe your experience with the open-eye meditation you just completed. Was it easier or more challenging for you than closed-eye meditations? Why do you think that is? What did you notice about your ability to keep a soft focus?

Was there a moment when you wanted to move your eyes to observe something else but remained steady in the practice? How did it feel to resist the distraction?

Did any memories come up for you during the meditation? Describe one of those memories.

Could you sense peace in your peripheral vision? Take a moment to reflect on something you're facing in your life today that feels intense. Is there peace somewhere within that intensity, too?

How might an unwavering stance of peace support you in your life right now? Could it help in your place of work or in a relationship you are in?

Set an Intention

When you find yourself in a situation that feels chaotic, become aware of the entirety of the scene that you are in. Although there is chaos in your foreground, look for something in the periphery that is peaceful.

Repeat these sentences three times:
"When I can find peace in the background, I remember there is always peace to be discovered. When I bring peace into my eyes, whatever doesn't feel peaceful softens around me."

PEACE IS A DAILY, A WEEKLY,

A MONTHLY PROCESS,

GRADUALLY CHANGING

OPINIONS, SLOWLY ERODING

OLD BARRIERS, QUIETLY

BUILDING NEW STRUCTURES.

John F. Kennedy

Free Your Mind

Meditation

1. Find a way to sit that feels grounding. If you are in a chair, move forward and plant both feet on the ground. If you're on the ground, you can sit on a pillow or against a wall to support your back.

2. Set a timer for ten minutes. Sitting tall, lengthen through the crown of your head and relax your shoulders. Soften your jaw and gently close your eyes.

3. Notice your breath flowing in and out of your body; allow it to flow without changing anything about it. Observe your breath as it flows in and out of you.

4. During this time, watch your mind as it moves through thoughts and emotions without any judgment. With a friendly attitude, say to yourself, "It's okay to feel this" and "It's okay to have this thought."

5. After recognizing that a thought or feeling has arisen, gently bring your awareness back to the in-flow and out-flow of your breath. For one to two minutes after the timer ends, let your mind relax. Let it feel free to be exactly as it is, whether alert or wandering, sleepy or impatient.

Writing Prompts

Is it easy or difficult for you to simply observe the present moment? Why do you think that is?

How did it feel when you allowed your feelings and thoughts to be present and adopted a friendly attitude toward them? Was this different from how you might normally think through your thoughts?

How has self-judgment hindered you in the past? Can you recall a recent or memorable example in which it has stopped you?

Do you think your work, relationships, or health would benefit from practicing friendliness toward your thoughts and emotions? In what way(s) would that be helpful?

What are three words you'd like your friends and family to use to describe you?

Set an Intention

Reflect on an intention that will inspire you
to attain inner peace this week. It could be as
simple as a single word or phrase, such as
"find the peace inside" or "breathe."

You might make a commitment to practice
the Free Your Mind meditation and use an
affirmation such as "I accept each moment, each
breath, each thought, and each emotion as it
comes with a welcoming attitude."

THE MOMENT THAT
JUDGMENT STOPS
THROUGH ACCEPTANCE
OF WHAT IS...

...YOU ARE FREE OF THE MIND. YOU HAVE MADE ROOM FOR LOVE, FOR JOY, FOR PEACE.

Eckhart Tolle

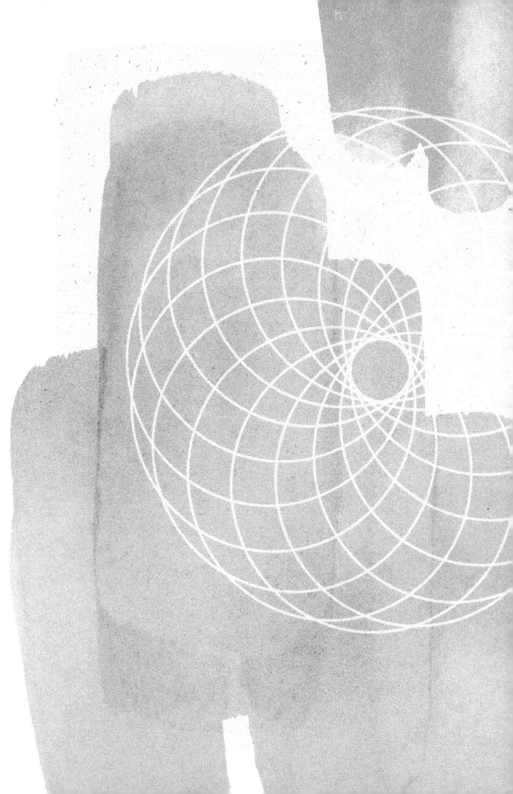

Part Two

FOCUS YOUR MIND

Sometimes life provides you with too many choices, and at other times it seems like you have no choice at all. When you focus your mind, you increase your ability to make a clear decision in a sea of options and uncover alternative pathways where you once thought there were none.

Focusing your mind also allows you to observe your thoughts and determine which ones are helpful and which ones move you further away from what you want in life. This awareness can help you reject unhelpful thoughts and learn how to cultivate beneficial thoughts, steering yourself toward the positive mind-set you need to find peace and calm in your day-to-day life.

FOR HIM WHO HAS

CONQUERED THE MIND,

THE MIND IS THE BEST OF

FRIENDS; BUT FOR ONE

WHO HAS FAILED TO DO SO,

HIS MIND WILL REMAIN

THE GREATEST ENEMY.

Bhagavad Gita

Count Your Focus

Meditation

1. Sit with relaxed shoulders, an upright back, and your chin parallel to the ground but tucked in slightly. Take a deep breath in and let it out fully. Settle into your restful but aware body posture.

2. Keep your eyes half open and let your gaze fall softly off the tip of your nose.

3. Become aware of your natural, unmanipulated breath. Begin to count your breaths. Count the inhale and exhale as one breath. Do not force the next breath to come, simply allow it to come naturally. Count ten full breath cycles, and then begin again.

4. If your mind wanders and you lose count, start again at one. Continue your focus on the count for three to five minutes.

5. Let go of the count and relax your mind. Allow your mind to relax for one or two minutes before opening your eyes and finishing the meditation.

Writing Prompts

Did you find it easy or difficult to keep count of your breaths? Did anything surprise you about the practice of focusing in this way?

Reflect upon the last few days—what has made it most difficult for you to focus? What action could you take that would benefit your focus when this distraction returns?

Can you recall any of the thoughts that distracted you during this practice? Are these recurring thoughts for you? From 1 to 100 percent, about how much of your energy do these thoughts typically occupy?

_____

_____

_____

_____

_____

_____

Reflect upon how it would feel if you could let go of thoughts that distract you daily.

_____

_____

_____

_____

_____

_____

If you could achieve laser focus this month, what are the three things you'd accomplish?

Set an Intention

It's okay if you've been distracted—it's normal and doesn't make you a bad person. You're human! With meditation and reflection, you can strengthen your mind.

Recognize a recent distraction that you regret has stalled you. Create an intention to not let this distract you for a specific, reasonable time frame. For example, if watching YouTube is your distraction, it's probably not reasonable to say you won't ever watch YouTube. Instead, you might set an intention such as "I will not watch YouTube from 9 a.m. to 5 p.m." or "I will not watch YouTube until I've done my report on XYZ."

DISTRACTION

WASTES OUR ENERGY;

CONCENTRATION

RESTORES IT.

Sharon Salzberg

Busy Mind Baggage

Meditation

1. Find a way to sit that feels grounding, so you can relax while remaining aware. Straighten your back—visualize your spine rooting into the surface beneath you and sprouting up beyond the crown of your head. Close your eyes and take a deep, restorative breath.

2. Let your breath follow its natural flow and bring your awareness to your inhales and exhales.

3. Imagine you are at the airport, about to go on an anticipated vacation. At the gate, you are told you must check all of your thoughts as baggage. As thoughts arise in your mind, imagine placing them into this checked baggage and return to your breathing. Keep going until your checked bags are filled with thoughts and your mind feels clear.

4. Give yourself a few minutes to sit and breathe without your thought baggage weighing you down. Notice if you feel lighter.

5. Imagine yourself reaching your vacation destination and discovering that your luggage full of thoughts has been repacked with gifts to enjoy on your vacation. How do you feel? Breathe into this feeling. Then, when you feel ready, open your eyes and smile.

Writing Prompts

How did it feel to have a container for your thoughts and how did it feel to be separated from them? Reflect on the meditation.

What did you notice about the thoughts you put in the baggage? Did you have to check a certain thought more than once? Did the stream of thoughts lessen in time?

Did this practice shine a light on a recurring thought that is negative or that doesn't make you a happier, more peaceful person? Reflect on what it might feel like if this thought or thoughts could remain "lost luggage." What might you accomplish without this thought?

Once you "checked your baggage," were there any deeper thoughts that arose? Describe your experience.

Is there something you haven't been focusing on recently that you'd like to? Reflect on the areas of your relationships, your work, your hobbies or creative pursuits, and your health.

Set an Intention

Set aside time in your week every day for an activity that helps you leave the busyness of your mind behind, even if it's for a short while. What will you choose to do? How long will you commit to doing it each day this week?

A GOOD PLACE TO START

IS WITH YOURSELF. SEE IF

YOU CAN GIVE YOURSELF

GIFTS THAT MAY BE TRUE

BLESSINGS, SUCH AS

SELF-ACCEPTANCE, OR

SOME TIME EACH DAY

WITH NO PURPOSE.

Jon Kabat-Zinn

Sensational Awareness

Meditation

1. Find a comfortable seated meditation position. Relax your face, your arms, and your belly, but keep an alert and long spine. Close your eyes and maintain your normal breathing.

2. Scan your body with your awareness, from the tips of your toes to the top of your head. Keep your body as still as possible and notice if you feel sensations in specific parts of your body.

3. When you notice a sensation, whether it is pleasurable or not, see if you can keep your awareness with it. Be curious about the sensation—what do you notice about it? Does it have a temperature? Can you visualize it as a color? Is it mild or intense? Is there tingling or another sensation? (Note: If you feel severe pain that might result in an injury if you remain still, adjust yourself; otherwise, please do your best to refrain from moving.)

4. Once you've taken inventory of a particular bodily sensation, imagine your inhale moving to the center of it. Notice if the sensation changes or dissipates as you exhale. For the next five to ten minutes, continue to investigate areas of your body where you feel sensations and take inventory of them. Send your breath to the center of each sensation.

5. Take one minute to relax the mind from awareness of sensations. Inhale deeply through your nose and then sigh out of your mouth. Open your eyes when you're ready.

Writing Prompts

Was it easy or difficult to keep stillness in the meditation? Describe your experience.

What did you notice about the sensations of your body? Were they subtle or loud? Did you notice anything about your body that you weren't aware of before?

Did intense sensations eventually disappear or change in some way? Reflect upon the changing nature of the sensations.

It's difficult to sit in discomfort. It is often the mind that wants to jump away, causing you to move and readjust your body. Is there a situation or conversation that you've been avoiding because it's uncomfortable for you? Take inventory of what that is and how it would feel to resolve it.

Expanding on the previous question, focus on your role in what you've been avoiding. What could you do to address it so that there is a beneficial and positive outcome for all involved? Reflect on what you can take personal responsibility for in the situation.

Set an Intention

Set an intention to resolve a task, situation,
or problem that you've been avoiding. Give
yourself a specific time frame for taking action.
Make sure this time frame is reasonable and
not pushed too far into the future.

THE MOST POWERFUL

RELATIONSHIP YOU

WILL EVER HAVE IS THE

RELATIONSHIP WITH

YOURSELF.

Steve Maraboli

Turn Down the Volume

Meditation

1. Sit comfortably with a tall spine. Loosen your shoulders and let them relax down your back. Close your eyes and find ease in this posture. Take a deep breath in and then let it go.

2. Notice the sounds in your environment. Start by noticing the most distant sounds you can hear. These sounds might be faint— it could be wind blowing through your neighbor's tree. Once you recognize a sound, allow your mind to move to another. Bring your awareness closer as you observe the sounds.

3. Notice the sounds of your body. Can you hear what's inside your belly? Can you hear the subtle sound of your breath? Without changing the pace of your breath, become aware of the sound of your breath as it moves in and out of your body.

4. Keep your focus glued to the sound of your breath. With full awareness of your environment of sounds, imagine there is a volume dial that you can turn up and down on everything outside of your breath. Turn the volume dial up on your breath. Become interested in your breath and its sound. Allow it to bring you inward. If you become distracted, imagine turning the volume down on the external distractions and come back to your breath, turning the volume up on it. Practice this for three to five minutes.

5. For the last minute or two, relax your mind. Let go of the need to focus, and be as you are. Open your eyes when you are ready.

Writing Prompts

Reflect on the meditation. Was there something new or interesting you noticed about your environment? Did you notice a sound you hadn't heard before?

Can you imagine a disturbing situation or place in which the practice of turning down the external volume would be helpful? Could it be possible to use the noise of your environment to bring you into deeper focus? Describe the situation or place you are thinking about and what it might look like to use the external noise in this way.

Recall a time when you had clear focus and flow. What were you doing? What do you remember about this time? Describe the place, the activity, how you felt, and anything you learned or accomplished with this focus.

If you could find focus in any environment, at any time, what are three things you'd benefit from either starting or completing (such as tasks, projects, contemplations, etc.)?

Who is the most focused person you know? Why do you believe they are so focused? What do you think helps them focus so effectively?

Set an Intention

Recall a person you know who has great focus. Write down three adjectives that describe their positive attributes. Using those adjectives, repeat this affirmation for yourself three times:

"I want to be a _____,

_____,

and _____ person.

With focus, I know I am unstoppable."

YOU CAN'T SAIL STRAIGHT INTO

THE WIND, AND IF YOU ONLY KNOW

HOW TO SAIL WITH THE WIND AT

YOUR BACK, YOU WILL ONLY GO

WHERE THE WIND BLOWS YOU. BUT

IF YOU KNOW HOW TO USE THE

WIND'S ENERGY AND ARE PATIENT,

YOU CAN SOMETIMES GET WHERE

YOU WANT TO GO.

Jon Kabat-Zinn

The Light of Awareness

Meditation

1. Sit comfortably on a chair or on the floor with a table in front of you. Place a candle on the table within arm's reach of where you are sitting. Adjust the height of the candle (or place a pillow underneath you to adjust your height) so that the wick of the candle is level with your upper lip. Light the candle and close your eyes for a moment.

2. Take a deep breath. As you exhale, open your eyes and gaze at the candle's flame. Do your best to keep your eyes open and unwavering for around fifteen seconds and up to one minute (maximum). When you need to blink, close your eyes.

3. For one to two minutes, keep your eyes gently closed and focus on any image or colors you see behind your closed eyelids. Relax with whatever you see until it fades away into darkness.

4. Open your eyes and repeat steps 2 and 3 two more times, holding your still gaze on the candle for up to one minute until you need to blink, and then closing your eyes and relaxing with the image you see in the dark of your closed eyelids.

5. After you have completed these steps three times, keep your eyes closed for a longer meditation, taking your focus to your natural inhale and exhale. Finally, relax your mind completely before you open your eyes and return from your meditation.

Writing Prompts

What was it like to hold your awareness on the candle flame and then on the image behind your closed eyelids? Describe any difficulties or surprises you discovered during the practice.

What qualities do you possess that you'd like to grow? Take a moment to shine light on three to five of your positive qualities.

Who has been a light in your life whom perhaps you haven't thought about or been in touch with for a while? Let the first person you think of be the one you reflect about. If you could tell them one thing right now, what would it be?

Describe a past experience, either a recent one or an older memorable one, where you have been impatient because you were overwhelmed or couldn't see the situation with focus. What is something you could do differently the next time you're faced with a similar situation?

It's not uncommon to dart focus from one place to the next, but in holding focus, a light can shine on previously unseen objects, feelings, situations, etc. Think about a recent interaction you had with someone and describe it here. What did you talk about? Why did you discuss this specific topic? Where were you when you had the conversation? What was the tone of the conversation? Then, contemplate: What part of the interaction was unseen to you? What don't you know about the other person? What struggles might they be having that are unseen? How are they more similar to you than you might've guessed?

Set an Intention

Let the light be a reminder to focus. The next time you are preparing for a task that requires great focus, create an environment that will set you up for success. Find a place where noise can be reduced or eliminated. Perhaps play soft music to help you focus. Light a candle or some incense to add to this environment and remind you of positive insights from your Light of Awareness meditation.

I AM IN THE WORLD FEELING MY WAY TO LIGHT "AMID THE ENCIRCLING GLOOM."

Mahatma Gandhi

Part Three

OVERCOME
OBSTACLES

Tibetan Buddhists pray for obstacles. They thrive on using problems to create positive mental states. You may wonder: How can obstacles be beneficial for creating a happier, more peaceful life? Obstacles are certainly difficult; it's normal to experience stress, anxiety, sleepless nights, and general unpleasantness in the heat of them. However, if your life was always in flow, you'd be complacent. You'd lack the ability to empathize with others, the motivation to find alternative ways of thinking or living, and the contrast necessary for gratitude.

The best way to move through an obstacle is to change the way you perceive it. When faced with a challenge, you can play one of two roles: the victim or the victor. If you choose to be the victor, you won't waste time looking for a person to blame, and you won't ask "Why me?" If you take on an obstacle knowing it will strengthen you, you'll be capable of taking on bigger challenges. When you can look at your obstacles as nourishment for your own advancement, you'll enrich your life and strengthen your mind. You might even find yourself cracking a knowing smile the next time you face adversity.

CHANGE THE WAY

YOU LOOK AT THINGS,

AND THE THINGS YOU

LOOK AT CHANGE.

Wayne Dyer

The Superhero in You

Meditation

1. Sit up tall in a relaxed position. Keep your chest open and relax your shoulder blades. Take a few deep breaths, then settle into your normal breathing pattern.

2. Bring to mind your favorite superhero or character of strength. If you have an angel, deity, or representation of divine strength that you look up to, it is also fine to bring this image into your mind. Imagine that this heroic, strong character is in front of you, and notice their stance, how they dress, the features of their face, and any other details your mind creates.

3. Think about the character or hero's biggest strengths and super-powers. In your mind, repeat this mantra at least three times: "May I be strong." See that the heroic character you pictured wants to support you and that they look kindly upon you.

4. Imagine that this character's strength and greatest attributes become a beaming ray of light. As you breathe, picture this light transferring to you, filling your body from the top of your head to the tips of your toes. Imagine being filled with all the strength and power that you admire in your heroic character.

5. Take five minutes to sit in this power and imagine moving through your day or approaching any obstacle with this inner strength. When you're finished, take a deep breath and sigh it out. Take this feeling with you throughout your day.

Writing Prompts

Describe an obstacle that you are currently facing.

Imagine that you are the superhero or powerful being you conjured in the Superhero in You meditation. Describe how they would approach your obstacle. What kinds of actions would they take? What might you imagine them saying?

If you could embody three of your superhero's best qualities, which would you choose?

Recall a memorable time when you felt like a hero or someone thanked you for doing something. Where were you? What were the circumstances? Who else was there?

When you were a child of five, six, seven, or eight years old, who did you look up to? It could be either a fictional character or a person who was in your life at the time. If there are multiple figures that come to mind, write them down. Try to recall a memory you have from that time with that person or character.

Set an Intention

Think of three adjectives that describe your superhero's most admirable qualities, then plug them into the sentence below and repeat the affirmation three times:

"I am a _____,

_____,

and _____ superhero.

There is no obstacle I can't overcome."

Repeat this affirmation throughout your day whenever you need a boost.

I THINK A HERO IS AN
ORDINARY INDIVIDUAL WHO
FINDS THE STRENGTH TO
PERSEVERE AND ENDURE IN
SPITE OF OVERWHELMING
OBSTACLES.

Christopher Reeve

Victory Mantra

Meditation

1. Sit upright in a posture that feels both relaxed and triumphant. Close your eyes and take a few deep breaths.

2. Bring your chin up just slightly higher than 90 degrees, so your face is pointing gently upward. Turn the corners of your lips up into a soft smile.

3. Repeat the word "victory" in your mind, like a mantra, again and again. Imagine the letters "V-I-C-T-O-R-Y" written behind your closed eyelids. Send your inhales and exhales to this image as if the breath could increase the energy of the word. Do this for three to five minutes.

4. Take one to two minutes to relax, and let go of the mantra. Sit in the energy of victory that you've created through your mantra repetition. Let your mind relax as you take in whatever sensations you are feeling.

5. Rub your hands together until you feel heat between them. Imagine that victory is in your hands. Bring your open palms to your face, to your neck, and to your heart, as if the heat of victory could saturate your skin. Take a deep breath and open your eyes.

Writing Prompts

How were you feeling before the start of the Victory Mantra meditation? How did you feel after the meditation?

What are some activities that you either do now or have done in the
past that make or have made you feel victorious? What is it about
those experiences that drums up victory for you?

When did you first learn about the idea of being victorious? Can you recall a victorious childhood memory in sports, academics, or another area of your life?

Is there a situation in your life today where you'd like to experience a victory? What would that look like for you? Can you think of a way that your victory would also be a victory for others involved?

_____

_____

_____

_____

_____

_____

Can you think of someone you know or admire in the media who victoriously overcame an obstacle? What about their victory do you admire the most?

_____

_____

_____

_____

_____

_____

_____

Set an Intention

Put an alert in your calendar for a random time
of day, for example 4:31 p.m. or 9:09 a.m., and
copy the Yogi Bhajan quote on the next page
into the event's subject line. You can make the
reminder repeat weekly for any amount of time
you like—try it for two weeks or ten weeks!

When the calendar alert pops up, read the
quote out loud and take a deep breath.
Remind yourself of your victorious nature.

WHENEVER YOU FACE ANYTHING AND
YOU DON'T HAVE AN ANSWER, JUST CALL
YOURSELF INSIDE AND SAY, "VICTORY."
LEAN ON "VICTORY." MAKE IT A GUIDE
WORD, MAKE IT A PRECIOUS WORD.
I DON'T KNOW WHAT YOU ARE, WHO
YOU ARE, WHY YOU ARE. DON'T ASK
QUESTIONS. DON'T DO YOUR ANALYSIS.
DON'T TRY TO SOLVE PROBLEMS. JUST
UTTER THE WORD "VICTORY." WITH JUST
THE MENTAL UTTERANCE OF THIS WORD
YOUR WHOLE LIFE WILL CHANGE.

Yogi Bhajan

Remember
Who You Are

Meditation

1. Sit in a posture that is comfortable, yet also alert. Let your shoulders roll open, giving your chest more space to expand with your breath. Take a few deep breaths, close your eyes, and settle in.

2. For one to two minutes, let your mind settle down by bringing your awareness to your breath. Feel your breath flow into and out of your abdomen.

3. Bring to mind a past struggle that was difficult for you but is now resolved. Let yourself recall it and experience in your mind how it was for you.

4. Contemplate in your meditation: What did you become after getting through this struggle? Stronger? More capable in some way? What new knowledge did you acquire? This experience grew you, helped you become who you are today. Recognize your own perseverance and strength.

5. Take as long as you'd like to sit with this recognition. This is who you are. On the other side of your struggle is greater strength. When you feel ready to end the meditation, inhale and then sigh deeply out of your mouth.

Writing Prompts

Describe the past struggle you imagined in the Remember Who You Are meditation. Who did you become after getting past this obstacle? What lessons did you learn?

_____

_____

_____

_____

_____

Make a list of your positive qualities. What do you like about yourself? What can you recognize about yourself? List at least twenty positive qualities.

_____

_____

_____

_____

_____

_____

_____

What is an obstacle you face today? What lesson do you think you'll learn once you overcome this obstacle?

Has someone made it known that they admire you, whether they've expressed that directly or indirectly? Think about someone who listens to you and learns from you. What do you think they admire about you?

What is something you don't necessarily enjoy in the moment, but that always makes you feel better afterward? Describe this experience.

Set an Intention

In the next twenty-four hours, do something
kind for yourself that you weren't already planning
to do. For example, you could go for a sauna or
a massage or watch your favorite movie.

"Something kind I will do for myself is:

_____."

YOU MAY ENCOUNTER MANY

DEFEATS, BUT YOU MUST

NOT BE DEFEATED. IN FACT,

IT MAY BE NECESSARY TO

ENCOUNTER THE DEFEATS, SO

YOU CAN KNOW WHO YOU

ARE, WHAT YOU CAN RISE

FROM, HOW YOU CAN STILL

COME OUT OF IT.

Maya Angelou

Your Resolve

Meditation

1. Sit in a posture that is comfortable, yet also watchful, and sharpen your mind. Soften your face. Close your eyes and take a few deep breaths.

2. Return your breathing to its natural, uncontrolled pattern. If your breathing seems rapid, let it be that way; if it seems slow, let it be slow. Spend a few minutes settling into a calm mental state, feeling your breath and allowing its unique rhythm to flow as it does unforced.

3. Bring your gentle attention to an obstacle you currently face. Observe the obstacle without a need to change it or judge it, just as you allowed your breath to be as it is.

4. Imagine yourself on the other side of this obstacle. Observe it as if you are watching a movie in which you overcome this obstacle. Create a resolve, an "I am" statement that embodies who you are on the other side of this obstacle. "I am _____ (POSITIVE ADJECTIVE)."

5. Repeat your "I am" statement three times in your mind, and then whisper it out loud three times. Sit with this feeling for as long as you like. When you're ready, open your eyes and take this feeling into your day.

Writing Prompts

Write down your "I am" statement from the Your Resolve meditation, as well as any reflections you have about what it means for you to be on the other side of the obstacle you identified. What is the first step you'll take toward overcoming this obstacle?

What are some other adjectives that describe how you aspire to be?
List ten of them here.

Look at the list of adjectives you wrote. Is there anyone in your life
today or in the past who comes to mind as possessing those qualities? How might they have become this way?

How could your learning from this obstacle be a pathway to help others facing a similar obstacle? Are there any real-world examples in which you can use the lessons you learned in this meditation to help others?

Can you think of any ways that you can already help others, even while you are in the midst of the obstacle you identified in this meditation? Reflect on your "I am" statement and some tangible contributions that this version of you can give to your family, friends, and communities.

Set an Intention

Start with the "I am" statement from the Your Resolve meditation and write three new ones, using three of the ten adjectives you listed. Replace "I am" with "You are" at the beginning of each sentence and write them on separate sticky notes. Put each note somewhere you'll find it in a time of need, like in your lunch container, in your laptop case, or on your coffee mug.

Write on one or two more sticky notes and place them someplace where a stranger might find them for inspiration. For example, you could put them inside a library book or on a restaurant table.

EVEN WHEN YOU THINK

YOU HAVE YOUR LIFE ALL

MAPPED OUT, THINGS

HAPPEN THAT SHAPE YOUR

DESTINY IN WAYS YOU MIGHT

NEVER HAVE IMAGINED.

Deepak Chopra

The Wisdom of You

Meditation

1. Sit upright in a restful way and straighten your spine. Soften your shoulder blades and relax. Let your eyes close and take a few deep breaths to release any tension.

2. Focus on your natural breath flow; imagine your mind's eye resting on top of your breath flowing in and out of your body. Take a few minutes to practice in this way, letting any thoughts that enter your mind be less interesting than your breathing. Let any thoughts you have roll away from you.

3. Imagine yourself in a beautiful garden where you meet a familiar face: a version of you as a child. You've caught your younger self playing in this garden. Notice what the younger you is playing with and wearing, as well as any other details that help create a vivid image. Come face-to-face with yourself.

4. Share any words of wisdom that come into your heart that this child-version of you needs to hear. Embrace yourself. Then, imagine that the child-you gives you an object. Take note of what it is and any details pertaining to it. With this object, this symbol of connection, the child-you also shares words of wisdom.

5. Take as long as you'd like to visit and embrace each other in your mind. When you feel ready, bring your hands to your heart, connecting to the wisdom you shared and letting it sink in. Take a deep breath in and sigh it out with a smile.

Writing Prompts

How old was the child-you that you imagined in the Wisdom of You meditation? What did you notice about what or how the child-you was playing? What is something positive you remember about that time in your life?

Reflect upon the words of wisdom shared between child-you and present-you. What did you share with the child-you, and what did the child-you share back? How might you apply this wisdom in your life today?

To whom do you look for wisdom? Maybe there are several people. Reflect upon who these people are and what you go to them for (e.g., career, health, financial, relationship, or spiritual advice).

Who was the most recent person to inspire you? What was the act they did that inspired you? Maybe they picked up trash from the ground in a park or raised money for a charitable cause. Why was this act inspirational to you?

Is there someone you can think of who might need support or inspiration? Think about a challenge they might be facing. What is something you could do to support or inspire this person?

Set an Intention

Recall the object that the child-you presented
to you in the Wisdom of You meditation. Set an
intention to find this object or a photo of this
object, or to create an artistic representation of
this object. Put the object or representation of it in
a special place to remind you of your own wisdom.

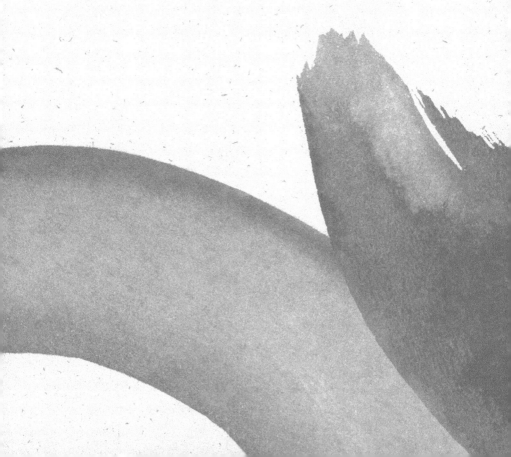

WE HAVE MOVED HORIZONTALLY FOR TOO LONG, NOW WE HAVE TO MOVE VERTICALLY. WE HAVE MOVED IN TIME FOR TOO LONG, NOW WE HAVE TO MOVE IN ETERNITY...

...WE HAVE DESIRED AND BEEN
AMBITIOUS FOR TOO LONG, NOW WE
HAVE TO DROP ALL DESIRING AND
AMBITION AND WE HAVE TO PUT OUR
WHOLE ENERGY INTO THE PRESENT
MOMENT, TO MAKE IT A CELEBRATION.

Osho

Part Four

FOSTER GRATITUDE
AND SPREAD JOY

When you tune in to the goodness of your life, you'll find even more goodness than you knew existed there. The rule is: Where attention goes, energy flows. Choosing to foster gratitude is the first step toward accessing your joy and spreading it.

Begin with gratitude for what you have today: your health, your family, your friends, etc. Then, expand your gratitude from there. Once you follow the same thread with family, friends, and every other facet of your life, you will be amazed at how much there is to be thankful for.

It's common to stress about what you don't have and to fall into "negativity bias." Don't accept this as your reality. With gratitude and compassion, you can change your mind about your life. As you focus on others, you'll spend less time focusing on the things you perceive are lacking from your life and instead cultivate your desire to give and care for others. In turn, you'll appreciate the most precious jewels of being: giving love, speaking with kindness, and doing good things for others. These are the most purposeful and fulfilling gifts you can give yourself, your community, and the world.

TEACH THIS TRIPLE TRUTH

TO ALL: A GENEROUS HEART,

KIND SPEECH, AND A LIFE OF

SERVICE AND COMPASSION

ARE THINGS WHICH

RENEW HUMANITY.

Seeds of Thankfulness

Meditation

1. Sit in a comfortable yet alert position, and release any tension in your shoulders, your jaw, and your brow. Take a deep breath in and sigh out of your mouth. Let your breathing relax into its natural rhythm.

2. Close your eyes. Bring to mind something or someone you're grateful for. Picture it clearly, complete the following statement with the first thing or person you think of, and repeat the statement in your mind: "I am grateful for _____."

3. Imagine that this gratitude is the seed of a beautiful flower. Visualize this seed being planted in a garden at your heart center. Send your breath to your heart, as if the breath could water this seed of gratitude.

4. Repeat steps 2 and 3 as many times as you like, bringing something or someone new to mind each time.

5. When you feel complete, imagine all the gratitude seeds you've planted sprouting up into incredible flowers. Imagine there is bright sunlight beaming upon you and this garden. Take a deep breath in through your nose and sigh it out of your mouth with a smile. Open your eyes when you're ready.

Writing Prompts

Describe your experience in the Seeds of Thankfulness meditation. Did anything come to mind that surprised you? What were you most happy about with the practice?

Take a look at a few important areas of your life: family, relationships, health, work, and personal passions. What are you most grateful for in each of these areas?

What do you want to create more of in your life? What is an action you can take to encourage this creation? (For instance, can you find a teacher, a mentor, a class, or a book—or is there a simple action you could complete—to add more of this good thing to your life?)

Recall a recent or prominent memory when you felt overcome with gratitude. Describe the experience: Who was there? What was happening?

What benefit do you see in having a formal daily practice of gratitude? What might that look like in your life?

Set an Intention

For the next week, at a set time each day,
either say out loud or write down three things
you are grateful for. You can set an alarm on
your phone or let a daily activity be the trigger for
you, like waiting for your morning coffee to brew.

If you enjoy the fruits of this practice,
make it an ongoing daily ritual.

BEING SATISFIED AND
GRATEFUL WITH WHAT WE
ALREADY HAVE IS A MAGICAL
GOLDEN KEY TO BEING ALIVE
IN A FULL, UNRESTRICTED,
AND INSPIRED WAY.

Pema Chödrön

Streaming Gratitude

Meditation

Do this practice either alone with a voice recording app or with a partner. If you have a partner, sit face-to-face with each other and have a timer nearby.

1. Begin by centering yourself with a deep and cleansing breath in, then sighing out of your mouth.

2. Start your voice recording app or, if you have a partner, start the timer. For ninety seconds, share what you are grateful for today. Do your best to speak without a filter and let your gratitude flow out loud as a stream of consciousness. If you are practicing with a partner, let each person speak for ninety seconds. The partner who is listening won't speak until the speaker's ninety seconds are up.

3. If you are practicing by yourself, at the end of the ninety seconds, say out loud, "Wow, I have a lot to be grateful for!" If you're practicing with a partner, the listening partner will say, "Wow, that's a lot to be grateful for!" After this, you will switch roles.

4. When you have completed the exercise, take a deep breath in and sigh it out of your mouth with a smile.

Writing Prompts

Did anything surprise you while you were listing things you are grateful for in the Streaming Gratitude meditation? Was it easy or difficult to fill ninety seconds with gratitude? Reflect on this.

What are some of the "small" things you are specifically grateful for today? List ten of them here.

Do you think the things you're grateful for have changed a lot over time? What do you remember being grateful for ten years ago? Five years ago?

Who is someone you are grateful for this week? This year? In your life? Who has been an angel to you or come to lend support to you at a crucial time?

_____

_____

_____

_____

_____

_____

Whether they have expressed it or not, who is someone that is grateful for you this week or this month? Reflect upon why they are grateful for you.

_____

_____

_____

_____

_____

_____

_____

Set an Intention

Gratitude wires your mind for positivity. Sharing gratitude helps someone else do the same, and your shared gratitude generates even more goodness. Set an intention to do the Streaming Gratitude practice with three different people this week.

GRATITUDE IS ONE OF
THE GREATEST MEDITATIONS
OF A LIFETIME, THE FASTEST
ATTITUDE UPLIFTER I KNOW.
BE GRATEFUL FOR ALL THE
GOOD IN YOUR LIFE AND
YOUR GOOD WILL ONLY
INCREASE, ALONG WITH
YOUR HAPPINESS.

Alan Cohen

Center of Your Heart

Meditation

1. Sit upright in a comfortable position that allows you to feel relaxed in your body.

2. With eyes open or closed, take a few slow deep breaths in and out, and then allow your breath to return to its natural rhythm.

3. Imagine that there is a light of gratitude and goodness at the center of your heart. Pick a color for this light and focus your attention on it as you breathe.

4. Think about the goodness and gratitude you have in your life. As you contemplate, visualize the light growing at your heart center. Watch this light expand to fill your entire heart, then your lungs, your torso, the upper half of your body, and then the lower half of your body, until it is beaming inside every part of your body. Breathe and imagine your entire body filled with this colorful light of gratitude and goodness.

5. Now, imagine that this light can beam out from you and fill the entire space where you sit. See it expand a mile out in all directions from you, then to the entire town or city where you are, the entire country, and the entire world. Sit for as long as you like, imagining the light of your gratitude shining across the globe.

Writing Prompts

Recall a time when you felt overwhelming gratitude—a time when you could've kissed the dirt with thankfulness. Was there a trigger? What was it? Describe your experience and how it felt.

Describe and reflect upon what has been the biggest gift of your life so far.

_____

_____

_____

_____

_____

_____

_____

If you could shine a light of love on a particular place or part of the world, where would it be? What draws you to this choice?

_____

_____

_____

_____

_____

_____

_____

_____

Who are some of the people you know you will come into contact with today? Can you write one or two things you're grateful for about each of these people?

If you could change the world with one wish, what would you wish for?

Set an Intention

Walk through your day as though you are wearing thankfulness glasses, becoming acutely aware of your gratitude for the people you encounter. Do your best to share what you are grateful for with them. See if you can share with a minimum of three people, and notice how that feels. Notice if it gets easier each time you share your gratitude with a different person.

THE VERY CENTER

OF YOUR HEART IS

WHERE LIFE BEGINS.

THE MOST BEAUTIFUL

PLACE ON EARTH.

Rumi

Loving Kindness

Meditation

1. Find a comfortable place to sit and begin to relax while remaining upright and tall through your spine. Take a deep breath in and out, centering yourself, and close your eyes.

2. Bring to mind three people: someone you hold very dear, some-one you've had a disagreement with or who annoys you, and someone you feel neutral about and don't know very well. Take a moment to get a clear image of each person and picture them standing next to one another.

3. All of these people have something in common with one another and with you. They all desire to be happy and free from suffering. Sit with this idea as you picture each person. Know that anything between you and them need not be resolved or argued right now. The idea of this exercise is to generate the awareness that, like you, they too want to be happy and feel loved.

4. Focus on each person individually. Give each of them the follow-ing blessing: "May you be happy, may you be healthy, may you be peaceful, may you be free from suffering and pain."

5. Imagine that each person receives this blessing from you and is better off because of it. Sit for as long as you like in the space of loving kindness, knowing that you've generated good for the people you identified, and feeling that if they could express it, they'd wish the same for you, too.

Writing Prompts

Was it difficult for you to share the blessing with each person in the Loving Kindness meditation? Why or why not? Were you able to visualize the blessing being given to you in return? Write down any interesting insights you have from the meditation.

With the person you have disagreed with or have found unfavorable, can you imagine that there might be more to the picture than you have been able to see? Reflect upon how this person desires to be happy, loved, and free from suffering, even if it doesn't seem obvious from their behavior.

Who did you choose as the person you feel neutral about? Might you have more in common with this person than you previously thought? What do you wish for this person?

What makes the people you chose for the meditation different from one another? Is there more that is different than similar or more that is similar about them than different? Does this bring up any insights about equanimity for you?

Are there any people in your life whom you may have overlooked who might be struggling or could use some encouragement? Name them here and reflect upon some kind sentiments you feel for each of them.

Set an Intention

Is there someone in your life whom you haven't forgiven or against whom you've held a grudge? Write them a forgiveness letter. You can choose to send it or not, but the important thing is to write it and make amends in your own mind.

REAL CHANGE IN THE

WORLD WILL ONLY COME

FROM A CHANGE OF HEART.

His Holiness the Dalai Lama

A Wish for Others

Meditation

1. Sit with a straight back in a comfortable yet confident way. Close your eyes and center yourself with your breath.

2. Imagine someone you know or have seen who is in pain or suffering. It could be someone close to you, someone you've never met, or even an animal. See their suffering in your mind and imagine how they might be feeling.

3. Generate a desire from within to take on their pain and alleviate their suffering. Know that you can handle it, and wholeheartedly wish that you could take their pain away.

4. Imagine the pain they feel could escape their body in the form of black smoke. As you inhale, breathe this black smoke out of their body and consciously choose to take it into your own heart. As the black smoke reaches your own heart, imagine that by taking it on, any of your own pain is smashed to pieces. As you exhale, see the blackness transforming into white light inside you, and breathe that white light out.

5. See this white light enveloping both you and the person whose pain you've taken on. Repeat this cycle as many times as you like, either with the same person or multiple people.

Writing Prompts

Describe your experience with the Wish for Others meditation. Did it feel good? Strange? Easy?

Who in your life do you wish you could see without suffering? Is there someone you don't know very well whose suffering you wish you could take on? Know that even generating this wish does a world of good in expanding your own heart.

Is there an act of kindness you can do for someone today? This week? Describe one or two actions you can take to lift someone's spirits.

Is there someone you've met who seems to embody selflessness? Who are they? Describe them and what you notice and admire about them.

Think about a unique gift that you possess. Are you good at connecting with others? At listening? Do you have a creative talent? Describe one of these gifts and how sharing this gift with others could be an act of service to increase their happiness. Who could you share it with?

Set an Intention

Set out to give your gift to the world as described in the last writing prompt on the previous page. It doesn't matter if you share it with one person or one thousand; take an action step today toward sharing this gift. Even if you can make one person's day 1 percent better, it's a worthwhile purpose. Set your sights on what you can give today, and set an intention to keep it growing tomorrow.

THEY MAY FORGET
WHAT YOU SAID...

...BUT THEY WILL NEVER
FORGET HOW YOU
MADE THEM FEEL.

Carl W. Buehner

CONCLUSION

Look back to where you were when you started this journal, and think about all that you've done since then—it has been a lot! I have no doubt that your commitment to practicing, reflecting, and doing the tough work has made a positive impact on your life. You might notice this impact in the way you interact with others with greater patience or understanding, or in patterns of yours that you hadn't fully recognized until now. These small achievements add up to a big difference. If you don't feel like you've got that magic "it" yet—surprise!—you're actually way closer than you think.

Meditation and self-inquiry are difficult. As Anne Lamott has famously said, "My mind is a bad neighborhood that I try not to go into alone." In this journey of being with yourself and looking at your mind and your thoughts, again and again, you've been facing whatever is there head-on. You've been accessing a place of stillness and compassion inside yourself by looking at what you may not have looked at or reflected upon before. This is the work of personal growth and gaining depth. It is a deep dive into the ocean of your being; it can be dark and scary under the surface, but there's three times as much life down there than there is above. How incredible that you're courageous enough to explore it in these practices!

Know that every moment you've spent reading, practicing the meditations, reflecting upon the prompts, and putting action into the intentions has created benefits within you and in your world. Recognize this work as a stepping-stone toward more fulfillment, purpose, and conscious living. Your active participation has laid a groundwork of well-being that, as you continue to grow it, will spread to others in your community who will be inspired by your process and your peace.

So, let's keep it going and develop your meditation practice further. Perhaps this is the year you take that bucket-list vacation in the mountains or find a meditation retreat to deepen your practice. You can also find a meditation community or a teacher near you who can help you learn more and deepen your experience. And with many online apps and courses just a click away, you can access an array of world-class teachers and resources to help you grow wherever you are. I've curated a list of my personal favorites for you in the following pages.

I leave you with this thought: Whatever path you choose, remain humble and remember kindness. There is an infinite amount to learn and a multitude of ways to look at anything. Stay open to that and hold yourself gently in the cacophony of it all.

RESOURCES

Here are some of my favorite resources for continuing your journey of inquiry and meditation.

APPS

Unplug Meditation (www.unplug.app/signup)—Unplug offers both in-studio and at-home meditations led by more than a hundred incredible teachers. The app includes video content that is polished and well curated, and most meditations last ten minutes or less. At their website, you can get a free week and 25 percent off your subscription with the code JORDANA.

Simple Habit (www.simplehabit.com)—This app has more than two thousand curated meditations from a wide variety of experts. Based on personal needs, you can get a meditation program designed just for you. Find me in this app and say hello! Use the code JORDANA on their website for a free week of meditations.

Peak Mindful (www.peakmindful.com)—An app for "performance" meditations, focused on productivity content and helping you hit the reset button while you're at work or on the go.

WEBSITES

Meditation School (www.davidgandelman.com/meditation-school)—
This is my favorite resource for diving deep into a meditation practice.
It offers live classes and workshops in addition to a members-only
area and access to engage one-on-one with spiritual advisors and
top-notch healers. Get 10 percent off a paid membership with the
code JORDANA.

Sounds True (www.soundstrue.com)—This site is led by teachers who
have been at the forefront of the consciousness movement. Here
you'll find podcasts, books, courses, and resources for every level.

Jordana.Love (www.jordana.love/shop)—On my site, you can try
the 100 meditations in 100 days program, which offers sixty-second
meditations meant to inspire you on a daily basis. If you're looking
for a more tailored approach, you can find different ways to work
with me one-on-one. Get 10 percent off any purchase with the code
SAYINGYES.

180 Retreats (www.180retreats.com)—Get out of your habitual patterns with a retreat that will change and enhance your life. Spiritual
retreats include hiking, meditation, yoga, sound healing, and more.

Evolved Leader Club (www.evolvedleader.club)—This is the ultimate
tool in mindfulness and flow for workplace leaders. A network of
leaders head the work with an inaugural 7-day trip to the base camp
of Mount Everest.

BOOKS

The Art of Forgiveness, Lovingkindness, and Peace by Jack Kornfield

Big Magic: Creative Living Beyond Fear by Elizabeth Gilbert

The Complete Beginners' Guide on How to Heal Chakras by Shiva Girish

Creative Visualization: Use the Power of Your Imagination to Create What You Want in Your Life by Shakti Gawain

Don't Hate, Meditate!: 5 Easy Practices to Get You Through the Hard Sh*t (and into the Good) by Megan Monahan

Fully Present: The Science, Art, and Practice of Mindfulness by Susan L. Smalley and Diana Winston

It's Not You, It's Me: How to Heal Your Relationship with Yourself and Others by Camilla Sacre-Dallerup

Making Life Meaningful by Lama Zopa Rinpoche

Meditation Made Easy by Lorin Roche

The Miracle of Mindfulness: An Introduction to the Practice of Meditation by Thich Nhat Hanh

Practical Meditation for Beginners: 10 Days to a Happier, Calmer You by Benjamin W. Decker

Radical Acceptance: Embracing Your Life with the Heart of a Buddha by Tara Brach

The Spontaneous Fulfillment of Desire: Harnessing the Infinite Power of Coincidence by Deepak Chopra

When Things Fall Apart: Heart Advice for Difficult Times by Pema Chödrön

The Wise Heart: A Guide to the Universal Teachings of Buddhist Psychology by Jack Kornfield

REFERENCES

Anonymous. *The Upanishads.* Translated by Juan Mascaro. New York: Penguin Classics, 1965.

Brach, Tara. "Trusting Ourselves, Trusting Life." October 7, 2015. https://www.tarabrach.com/trusting-ourselves-trusting-life-2/.

Chödrön, Pema. *Good Medicine: How to Turn Pain into Compassion with Tonglen Meditation.* Sounds True, Inc, 2001.

Kabat-Zinn, Jon. "This Loving-Kindness Meditation Is a Radical Act of Love." November 8, 2018. https://www.mindful.org/this-loving-kindness-meditation-is-a-radical-act-of-love/.

"The Mindfulness of Breathing." Accessed January 17, 2020. https:// thebuddhistcentre.com/text/mindfulness-breathing.

Swami Muktibodhananda. *Hatha Yoga Pradipika.* Bihar School of Yoga, 1998.

ACKNOWLEDGMENTS

To my teachers and mentors (Rabbi Lori Shapiro, Ajay Chhetri, Govind Das, Shiva Girish, Sam Delug, Venerable Robina, and Lama Zopa Rinpoche), for kindness and generosity in sharing knowledge that enriches my life and the lives of many.

ABOUT THE AUTHOR

Jordana Reim has dedicated her life to expanding consciousness—her own, her community's, and humanity's. Before writing this book (her first!), she spent many years refining her personal practice through travel, study, and residencies at some of the most sacred and beautiful places on Earth, including the islands of Thailand, ashrams of India, and Himalayas of Nepal. On a continual search for higher ground, the New Jersey native shares her learning by coaching others in corporate, group, and private meditation, breathing, and other wellness modalities in Los Angeles.

A believer in the wisdom of reconnecting humanity with nature's beauty and power, Reim has led annual trekking retreats from all over the world since 2018 to Nepal, Bhutan, and ultimately to the base camp of Mt. Everest, through her company, 180 Retreats.

In 2020, Reim launched the podcast "A Minute to Meditate," premised on her conviction that small positive changes over time create huge shifts in fulfillment and happiness. In her previous career, Reim was an award-winning producer of advertising in New York City.

Reim resides in Santa Monica, California, and keeps a pied-à-terre in Kathmandu, which is more practical than it sounds, given her frequent travels there.

CPSIA information can be obtained
at www.ICGtesting.com
Printed in the USA
JSHW011119280420
5343JS00005B/7